D1809729

**Map Of The World By Jodocus Hondius, 1611**

# MAP OF THE WORLD

## BY JODOCUS HONDIUS
## 1611

EDITED BY

**EDWARD LUTHER STEVENSON, Ph.D.**

AND

**JOSEPH FISCHER, S.J.**

# MAP OF THE WORLD

## BY JODOCUS HONDIUS
## 1611

EDITED BY

**EDWARD LUTHER STEVENSON, Ph.D.**

AND

**JOSEPH FISCHER, S.J.**

**facsimile**

ISSUED UNDER THE JOINT AUSPICES OF

### THE AMERICAN GEOGRAPHICAL SOCIETY

AND

### THE HISPANIC SOCIETY OF AMERICA

**NEW YORK**
**1907**

TO

HIS HIGHNESS

PRINCE MAX VON WALDBURG ZU WOLFEGG-WALDSEE

RESPECTFULLY DEDICATED

BY THE EDITORS

I

The Hondius world map as it appeared when found, *circa* 1

# FOREWORD

IT was in 1507 that Martin Waldseemüller (Ilacomilus) issued his great world map, the *Cosmographia universalis*, the first map bearing the name AMERICA. In presenting at this time, 1907, to the friends of historical geography this reproduction of the last and greatest work of Jodocus Hondius, it is not inappropriate to refer to it as a publication commemorating the four-hundredth anniversary of that event.

Like the Waldseemüller map, this cartographical masterpiece of Hondius, it appears, has been preserved in but one copy. Every effort to find a second copy has been without avail (*vide* p. 14).

The map was found by Professor Joseph Fischer, S. J., of Feldkirch, Austria, in the same year, 1901, and in the same castle, Wolfegg, Württemberg, Germany, in which the Waldseemüller maps of 1507 and 1516 were found. Bound in substantial board cover, the maps of Waldseemüller were well preserved; the condition of the Hondius map was such as to make its reproduction in serviceable form appear almost impossible. (See Fig. I.)

Mounted on coarse linen and attached to heavy oak rollers, it was found, with other old material, in the attic of the castle. By reason of the large folds of the linen, and the many loose and torn sections, it was with very great

. 5

difficulty that one could either trace the outlines or decipher the text of the map, notwithstanding its size (246 by 160 cm.). Without doubt, its complete destruction would have followed within a comparatively short time. It was only natural that those who visited the castle should wish to see this document of such great importance, but each unrolling meant its further damage. While on a visit to Wolfegg, the distinguished librarian of the Vatican, Dr. Franz Ehrle, S. J., after a careful examination of the map, expressed a willingness to undertake its removal from the coarse linen backing, to clean and restore it, so far as possible, and to mount it on thin paper. To this suggestion the Prince willingly gave his assent. The map was carefully packed and sent to Rome, where, in the atelier of Dr. Ehrle, and under his careful supervision, it was removed, piece by piece, from the old mount, and the original eighteen parts were remounted on white paper. These restored sheets were then attached by gelatin strips to cardboard, and the whole neatly and substantially bound. Encased in a handsome strong box, it has now its place in the collection of engravings in the library of the Prince, one of the richest and most extensive collections of engravings to be found in private possession in all Europe. For the excellent work done by the distinguished librarian of the Vatican, and the service he has rendered the science of historical geography, it is fitting that profound thanks should here be expressed.

Manifesting the same willingness and interest that was shown in the reproduction of the Waldseemüller maps, His Highness Prince Franz von Waldburg zu Wolfegg-Waldsee, before his lamented death, in 1906, gave his consent for the publication of this map, thus most graciously placing all those who are interested in cartographical science under lasting obligations. His son and successor, the present reigning Prince Max von Waldburg zu Wolfegg-Waldsee, has expressed the same interest in the undertaking, and to him this reproduction is dedicated.

The photographic negatives of the map, made in Feldkirch by the photographer Alois Gnädinger under the direction and constant supervision of Professor Gottfried Richen, S. J., were sent to Mr. Edward Bierstadt, New York City, and in his establishment, which is distinguished for the excellence of its work, the map has been artistically reproduced, faithful to the original in every detail. The printing of the map and of the descriptive text has been under the supervision of Professor Stevenson. The expense of the undertaking is jointly carried by The American Geographical Society and The Hispanic Society of America. To these societies the editors here express their cordial thanks.

It is fortunate that the outlines and the legends of the map are little injured. While the missing parts of the pictorial ornamentations, and of the two large legends in particular, might easily have been restored, in the interest of science it was thought this should not be done. To afford a clearer conception of the whole to those who have not the privilege of examining the original, we have added this brief explanatory and descriptive text. Notwithstanding the small scale, Fig. I is sufficiently large to show the condition of the map before it was detached from the coarse linen. It is interesting to note that labels had been pasted on the map bearing such names as Washington, Baltimore, Philadelphia. Evidently the map did service in geographical instruction when its information was found not to be up to date.

For information kindly furnished concerning Jodocus

7

Hondius and his activity as a cartographer, we are indebted to Dr. Ferdinand van Ortroy, Professor of Geography at the University of Ghent, and also to Professor Franz von Wieser, of the University of Innsbruck.

To the many librarians, and to the many professors interested in historical geography, from whom much assistance has been received, the sincere thanks of the editors are here expressed.

# THE LAST GREAT WORLD MAP
## OF JODOCUS HONDIUS[1]

ACROSS the upper border of this map, which presents
the world in two great hemispheres, appears its
title in large capital letters: *"NOVISSIMA AC
EXACTISSIMA TOTIUS ORBIS TERRARUM
DESCRIPTIO MAGNA."* In well drawn minuscules
this inscription continues in the second line: *"cura & indus-
tria ex optimis quibusᴣ tabulis Geographicis et Hydro-
graphicis nuperrimisᴣ doctorum virorum observationib?
duobus planisphaerijs delineata Auct. J. Hondio."* It is
here expressly stated that Jodocus Hondius is the author.

Concerning his earlier cartographical activities he gives
us information on the last sheet. Hondius here explains
the requisites of a map constructed for mariners, like the
one which Mercator was the first to draw (*vide* the great
world map *ad usum navigantium* of 1569), and also

---

[1] The first announcement of the
discovery of the map was made by
Professor Fischer in a paper on *"Die
kartographische Darstellung der Entdeckungen der Normanen in Ame-
rika,"* at the Fourteenth International
Congress of Americanists in Stutt-
gart, 1904. *Vide* the Official Report
of the Congress, Vol. I, p. 31, *seq.*
A reference to the map may also be
found in *Stimmen aus Maria-Laach,*
*"Von Alten Karten,"* Bd. 71, p. 352,
*seq.*, 1906.

A reproduction of the map in size
of the original was first exhibited at
the Fifteenth International Congress
of Americanists in Quebec, 1906, by
Professor Stevenson. *Vide* the Official Report of the Congress.

the requisites for one constructed merely for purposes of illustration. Following the example of his countryman Mercator, he had earlier published a number of world maps as well as many separate maps of the four continents, "*artificio insuper directionum apte constituendarum mechanice et plane addito explicatoque*," which many later seem to have copied. As opinions differed concerning the Mercator projection, because of the great expansion of the land near the two poles, made necessary by the peculiar character of the construction, Hondius, to avoid these errors, chose to represent the earth in hemispheres, as he had done in a former instance; but for this map he chose a larger scale. It was not without great care and industry, as he says, that he undertook to indicate on his map as accurately as possible every region which had been discovered and explored within in recent times. From the explicit data here given, which throw much new light on the cartographical activities of the author, it is evident that the map owes its origin to the Jodocus Hondius who died in 1611.[1] On sheets 13 and 14 we find a legend, giving the place in which the map was printed: "*Amsterodami Excufum in aedibus Judoci Hondij. Ghedruckt in der Calverstraete in den Wackeren Hondt by het Stadthuys.*"

That we have here to do with the last great work of that master appears certain from the sources of which he clearly made use in its execution, sources giving the results of the

[1] Concerning Jodocus Hondius and his other cartographical activities, *vide* the Introduction to the various editions of the large and the small Atlases by Mercator-Hondius; also Wauwermann, "*Histoire de l'école cartographique Belge et Anversoise du XVIe siècle*," 2 Vols., Bruxelles, 1895; J. van Raemdonck, "*Gerhard Mercator, sa vie et ses œuvres*," St. Nicolas, 1869; "*Biographie Nationale, publiée par l'Académie Royale des sciences de Belgique*," Vol. V, Bruxelles, 1876; A. E. v. Nordenskiöld, "*Facsimile Atlas*," Stockholm, 1889; by the same author, "*Periplus*," Stockholm, 1897.

different voyages of discovery of 1608, as for example, the voyage to the north coast of North America which the Englishman Weymouth had undertaken along the river Baixos, for a distance of 75 German miles, *"si modo fluv. sit et non fretum."*[1] Hondius indeed knew of a voyage which had been undertaken in 1609 by way of "Nova Semla" (Nowaja Semlja) to China, but which had proved unsuccessful.[2] It seems very evident that the map could not have been completed before the end of 1610. On the 16th of February, 1611, Jodocus Hondius died, at the age of forty-eight, after an illness lasting four days.

Whether the master ever saw this last great work complete, with all that contributes to its remarkable character, whether he had the oversight of its publication, we do not know. That we have it in essentially the same condition as drawn by Hondius is in part assured by the fact that the discoveries of Hudson (Hudson's Bay, Hudson's Strait) which should have become known in Amsterdam as early as 1613, where the map was published, are not indicated. There appears, however, in South America one indication that the map as we know it, was altered at a later date; it is

[1] George Weymouth, as Peschel has noticed (*"Geschichte der Erdkunde,"* 2d edition, revised by Sophus Ruge, München, 1877, p. 304), claimed to have sailed *"75 deutsche Meilen* (100 leagues) *West bei Süd in der* (*später sog.*) *Hudsonstrasse. Jede neuere Karte straft eine solche Behauptung Lügen, aber da wir Weymouth's Logbuch nicht besitzen, sondern nur den Bericht des ungenauen Purchas* ('Pilgrims,' tom. III, London, 1626, fol. 809), *so lässt sich noch nicht entscheiden, ob der Seefahrer Weymouth, wofür man ihn gewöhnlich hält, ein Schelm gewesen sei."* Peschel-Ruge would now also consider him a cheat, since Hondius at least sixteen years before Purchase, had made mention of the seventy-five German miles. The voyage took place, however, according to the usually accepted account, not in 1608, but in 1602. The logbook of George Weymouth came, through the mediation of a Dutch savant, Peter Plancius, in 1609 into the hands of Henry Hudson.

[2] On sheet 5, at the conclusion of a long legend concerning voyages to Nova Semla, we read, *"Anno vero 1609 denuo eo navigatum est, sed re infecta redierunt."* Evidently the ref-

the legend "Lamayrs Passage." We find, it is true, not only the Le Maire Strait but also the *"Staten Land"* and *"de Eylanden van Barnevelt,"* cartographical data which owe their origin to the Dutch expedition of Le Maire and van Schouten (1615–1617), on Blaeu's globes, globes which bear the explicit inscription, "Guilhelmus Janssonius Blaeu 1599,[1] 1602."[2] Fischer found recently in the Royal Bavarian Army Library a small world map (*"Nova totius terrarum orbis geographica ac hydrographica descriptio"*) with the legend, *"Petrus Kaerius Flander celavit et excudit Amsterodami anno a nato Christo 1608,"* on which the *"Lameers Straet"* is represented. Nevertheless it appears to us that in this and in similar instances we have to do with later insertions or with typographical errors, 1608 for 1618. The *"Lameers Straet"* is likewise to be found, without the *"Staten Land"* and the other discoveries of Le Maire, on a world map of Joannes Jansonius (*"Orbis terrarum descriptio duobus planis hemispheriis comprehensa"*) of the year 1618, which is likewise in the Royal Bavarian Army Library.

erence here is to a voyage which was undertaken by Henry Hudson in the service of the Dutch East India Company on which, in his yacht, *The Halfmoon,* he had made a second attempt to break through the ice barriers in search of a northeast passage. As a result of Hudson's attempt in 1608, we find that Hondius has recorded on his map, sheet 3, in latitude 80, the legend, *"Glacies ab Hudson detect(a) anno 1608."* As, however, he arrived in the extreme north near the first of May, he came upon great ice masses, and was thus prevented from sailing beyond Nova Semla. Suddenly changing his plans, he turned about and began his search for a northwest passage, to undertake which the account of Weymouth gave him encouragement. Comp. Sophus Ruge, *"Geschichte des Zeitalters der Entdeckungen,"* Berlin, 1881, p. 515; G. M. Asher, *"Henry Hudson, the Navigator,"* London, 1860, p. 44. Concerning the voyages of discovery of Hudson in the years 1609–1611 no reference is to be found on the Hondius map.

[1] Comp. P. T. H. Baudet, *"Leven en werken van Willem Jansz. Blaeu,"* Utrecht, 1871, p. 43 *seq.*

[2] This globe was found by Professor Fischer in the Museum of the city of Schaffhausen.

12

It is interesting to note that while our map, sheet 14, makes mention only of the four explorers who had circumnavigated the globe: Ferdinandus Magellanes, Franciscus Dracus, Thomas Candysh, and Olivarius van der Nort, Jansonius cites in addition, as one who had sailed through the Strait of Magellan, J. Spilberg, who *"superiore anno, qui fuit 1615, ingressus est illud."* [1]

That the map as we have it with the entry [2] "Lamayrs Passage" may not have been published before 1618, finds confirmation in the circumstance that in that year (1618) Jodocus Hondius, [3] oldest son of our author, published in Amsterdam a description of the map, containing nineteen pages, *"Amstelodami. Excudebat Jodocus Hondius, sub signo Canis Vigilantis in Platea Vitulina, prope Senatoriam Domum, Anno 1618."*

Whether we have a reference here to a text by the author of our map, or to an independent publication of the son,

[1] Georg v. Spilbergen (or Spilbergt) left Texel August 8, 1614, as commander of six vessels and sailed through the Strait of Magellan. On the 20th of September, 1616, Le Maire and van Schouten came up with him in their ship *Concordia*, after sailing around the southern point of America (Le Maire Strait, Cape Horn). Le Maire died on the return voyage. On July 1st, 1617, Spilbergen sailed into his home port. *Vide "Speculum Orientalis Occidentalisque Indiae navigationum; Quarum una Georgij à Spilbergen classis cum potestate Praefecti, altera Iacobi le Maire auspicijs imperioque directa, Annis 1614, 16, 16, 17, 18,* Lugd. Batav. 1619." In the same year there appeared two other notices of the voyage in Amsterdam and Leiden.

[2] That the Le Maire Strait was later inserted may be explained through the fact that such an alteration could easily be made in the map, and that the expedition had gone out from Holland.

[3] Petrus Montanus, the brother-in-law of Hondius, expressly states in his various editions of the large Atlases, which were issued after 1611, that, of the nine children of Jodocus who survived him, the oldest bore the same name as the father, i.e., Jodocus. As this important fact has repeatedly been overlooked, the most contradictory statements have been made concerning the family of Hondius and the year of his birth. He was born in the year 1563. Of his thirteen children, seven sons and six daughters, four sons died before the father. The

who was less distinguished as a geographer and cartographer, we are unable to say.

In a paper written by Professor George Davidson, of the University of California, and published by the California Historical Society,[1] attention is called to a copy of the text above referred to and to a copy of the map printed in the year 1627. Both text and map, which were in private possession, were destroyed in the great San Francisco fire of April, 1906. This destruction is greatly to be deplored as the map is reported to have been in an excellent state of preservation. No other copy of the map has been found, and it seems that there is nowhere reference to it in cartographical literature. On the copy referred to by Professor Davidson a second son of Jodocus Hondius, Henry by name, was mentioned with the inscription, *"Amstelodami. Excutum apud Henricum Hondium, habitans supra Damum sub insigno* [sic] *Atlantis. Anno 1627."*

The chief significance of this world map, so fortunately preserved in the Castle Wolfegg, lies in the fact that we have in it the world represented as a great cartographer like Hondius thought it should be done, based on the results as they were known in 1611, and that we are now in a position, through comparison of the work of Hondius with the great world maps of Waldseemüller of 1507 and 1516, to see clearly the progress in map-making within one hundred years. That the advance was most remarkable is evident. Especially is this to be seen in the case of Amer-

names of the surviving sons were Jodocus, Henry (usually called Henry the younger, to distinguish him from his uncle, Henry the elder) and William. All were distinguished as engravers, and the first two as cartographers.

[1] Professor George Davidson, "*The Identification of Sir Francis Drake's Anchorage on the Coast of California in the year 1579*," California Historical Society Publication, San Francisco, 1890, p. 41.

ica, but it is interesting to note the name *Berlin* on the Waldseemüller maps which Hondius omits.

The exaggerated representation of cannibals in Brazil on the *Carta Marina* of 1516 is still more exaggerated by Hondius. Greenland is less accurately drawn than by Waldseemüller, or by Canerio whom Waldseemüller practically copied. The incorrect position of the "Forbisher Straits" is due to the error of the explorer Frobisher (1576–1578). The large island *Frisland,* and *S. Thomae coenobium* in Greenland are taken from the Zeno map, whose other errors Hondius fortunately avoided. It is remarkable that the influence of the Caludius Clavus map (*cir.* 1420) made itself felt in the nomenclature of Greenland on the Hondius map as it had on the maps of Waldseemüller, and it is still more remarkable that the influence of the Ulm Ptolemy, so far as Asia and Africa are concerned, extended over Waldseemüller and Mercator to Hondius. The same erroneous references by Waldseemüller to Ethiopia in South Africa[1] we find on the Hondius map, as Adia, Garna instead of Garma, Vigiti magna, etc. From what sources Hondius, however, took these and similar errors is not easy to determine. So far as they may be found on the sea chart of Mercator (and the majority of them are there given), it is probable that they may have been taken from that epoch-making production.

We can not attempt to give here all the sources which Hondius may have consulted. This must be reserved for a special investigation, as must also a detailed consideration of the great geographical and historical value of the map and its relation to other maps of the period.

[1] That Waldseemüller fell into this erroneous representation through the use of a special map of Abyssinia of the middle of the 15th century, Fischer has been able to determine through the discovery of three different recensions of that map which he proposes soon to publish.

Only this much need be further said concerning his sources, that the most important explorations of that time, as the circumnavigation of the globe by Drake and Cavendish, the exploration of Guyana by Raleigh, and also the discoveries of Davis, had already been cartographically represented by Hondius. The most important cartographical results of the explorations of the Dutch into the ice regions of the north he took from the *"Delineatio cartae trium navigationum per Batavos ad septemtrionalem plagam Norvegiae, Moscoviae et novae Semblae"* of Wilhelm Barents (1588).

Through these voyages of discovery, together with the discoveries by Hudson along the east coast of Greenland, likewise recorded by Hondius, an end was made to the erroneous representations of the Northland, as it had been established by Mercator's marine map of 1569. In like manner great service was rendered to cartography by Hondius in that he brought into prominence the results of the explorations of Drake along the southwest coast of South America. In the maps of Mercator and Ortelius, that coast was made to run toward the northwest instead of toward the northeast, as was correctly demonstrated by Drake.

Hondius made use not only of cartographical sources but also of written data. Almost every sheet of the map serves to illustrate this fact. Of the many examples, but one need here especially be cited, as it acquaints us with Hondius' method of work, and emphasizes a characteristic peculiarity which serves to indicate the influence of the map. On the 11th sheet he rightly expresses the opinion that Mercator, influenced by the information which owed its origin to Marco Polo, had given the northern part of Asia a too great extension northward. This he had the more readily done as China, according to the information of Jesuits with whom Mercator was acquainted, extended to parallel 52 north latitude. Against this supposition, however, were the determinations of latitude made later with the astrolabe by the Jesuit Jacobus Pontoius, who in the year 1602 gave the latitude of the capital Papin (Peking) as 40 degrees, which is quite correct, and he made the north of China terminate in latitude 42. He further remarked that north of China there were no peoples of any importance, nor any provinces except Loxam. Perplexed over this matter, Hondius undertook to test anew the account of Marco Polo, and, as a result, constructed his erroneous map of Northeast Asia, differing considerably from his first one. It was in consequence of this innovation that the Anian Strait, which had been marked by every one after 1566, was omitted. After 1630 the new idea was gradually accepted, but the origin of the error, so far as we know, is not found on any other map.

An especial merit Hondius claims for himself on sheet 18: that he was the first to represent the currents of the ocean, and the winds which blow constantly in one direction throughout the year, or at any rate through certain seasons of the year. On these points the data of the map are interesting: as for example, in the Atlantic Ocean *"Subsolanus continuo flat inter utrumque Tropicum in mari aperto del Nort"*; east of Florida, *"Northoost ten Oost"* (*Courrant*); south of New Foundland, *"Noord-Oost Courrant"*; in *Fretum Davis, "West C."*; southeast of Greenland, *"West Courrant."* In an artistic cartouch which appears on sheet 14 is a lengthy legend which gives information concerning the direction of the winds in the Pacific Ocean and along its coast regions, and the significance of these winds for the mariner. Since Hondius himself assigns no special merit

17

to the *"Directions Spiralen,"* mention need be made here only of the fact that he made use of the windrose with its thirty-two points, and that his first meridian passes through the islands of S. Maria and S. Michael, the *"Insulae Flandricae, alias Açores Insulae,"* because in these islands no variation of the magnetic needle occurs, as he expressly declared in his large Atlas, and also indicates the same on this map by the legend, *"Inter Flores et Fayl I. nulla est deviatio acus."* In five other places of the Atlantic Ocean, and in many places in the north of Europe, Hondius gives express information concerning the behavior of the magnetic needle.

Justice would not be done the author as a map-maker or as an engraver were reference not made to the artistic ornamentations of this great work. As the world map of Waldseemüller is of great significance by reason of its artistic merit, being the first large map engraved on wood, so this map of Hondius has a well justified claim to admiration as a copper engraving.

"For adornment and for entertainment," he says, on sheet 18, he has represented the various animals which are useful to man, the lord of creation. He has added, Noah and his children and grandchildren and the list of the nations which descended from them, as best he could after a study of the various learned authors. There are many large pictures on the map, as the Fall of Man, the Giving of the Law on Mount Sinai, and other representations which for the history of art are not without great significance. In conclusion it may be pointed out that we have on sheet 17 the portrait of Gerhard Mercator and that of the author of the map, as appears from a comparison of Fig. II. The woman, it is probable, was intended to represent the wife of Hondius, and the two young men his sons Jodocus and

18

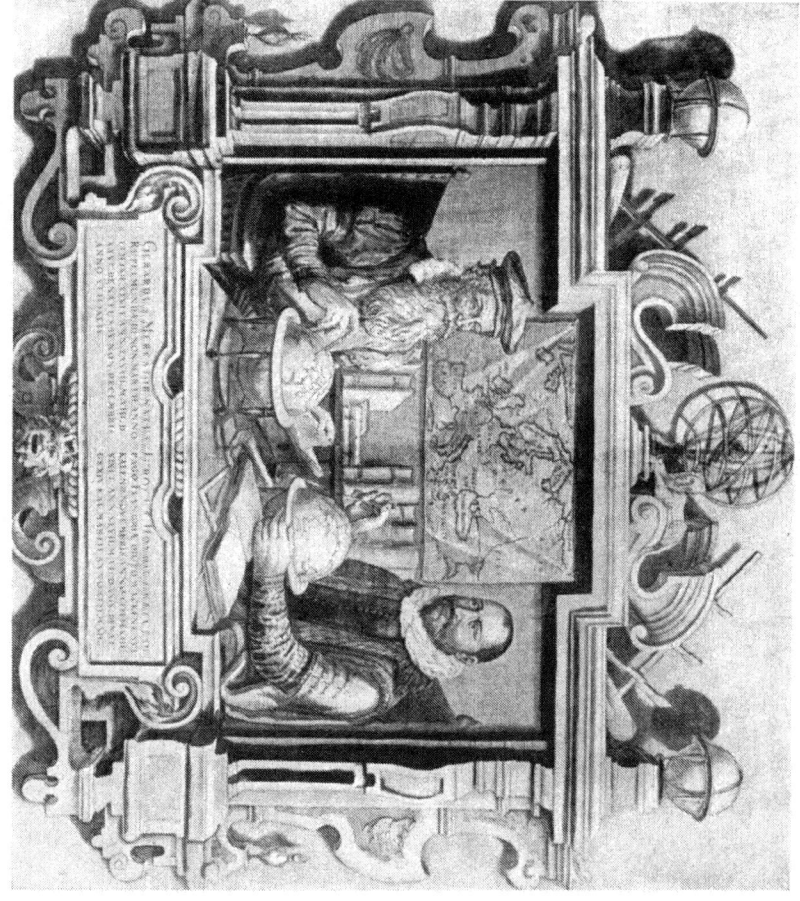

Gerardus Mercator and Jodocus Hondius

Henry, who are expressly mentioned as exercising the art of their father, *"Artem patris profitentur."*

Although Jodocus Hondius as geographer and cartographer was not so distinguished as Gerhard Mercator, and as engraver not so famous as his son Henry, yet he completely fulfilled the great expectations which he aroused even when only a child of eight years, and secured for himself an honorable place among the masters as geographer and cartographer.

To a proper estimate of his services this reproduction of his great world map makes special contribution.

*"Vale amice lector et fruere"* (sheet 18).

S

⑤

A00001369²193

Lightning Source UK Ltd.
Milton Keynes UK
UKHW022014080321
380016UK00005B/913